HAL LEONARD

RECORDER METHOD

BY SARAH JEFFERY

CONTENTS

ISBN 978-1-70518-420-2

To access audio and video visit:
www.halleonard.com/mylibrary

Enter Code
1334-1352-8963-5741

Visit Hal Leonard Online at
www.halleonard.com

World headquarters, contact:
Hal Leonard
7777 West Bluemound Road
Milwaukee, WI 53213
Email: info@halleonard.com

In Europe, contact:
Hal Leonard Europe Limited
Dettingen Way
Bury St Edmunds, Suffolk, IP33 3YB
Email: info@halleonardeurope.com

In Australia, contact:
Hal Leonard Australia Pty. Ltd.
4 Lentara Court
Cheltenham, Victoria, 3192 Australia
Email: info@halleonard.com.au

INTRODUCTION

Welcome to the *Hal Leonard Recorder Method.* This method has been designed to help you accomplish your goal of becoming a proficient recorder player. You'll learn how to make a good sound, finger notes, and play famous popular songs alongside classic and new, original recorder repertoire. Every chapter also includes an **OVER TO YOU** section that will guide you through the first steps of improvisation and composition. This book doesn't just teach you how to play notes on the page; we are going on a journey to become well-rounded and joyful musicians.

Every stage of learning is accompanied by a video lesson tutorial, helping to introduce new concepts in a fun and accessible way. Each video includes both recorder and aural technique, essential facets of music-making. You can continue to refer back to these at any stage in your learning and use them as general warm-ups to your practice at home. The *Hal Leonard Recorder Method* has everything you need to jump into the world of the recorder with confidence and success!

VIDEO LESSONS AND AUDIO

Whenever you see a video icon, play the corresponding tutorial lesson. This book also comes with accompanying audio, featuring backing and demonstration tracks of select exercises and tunes within the lessons. You'll see an audio icon when a track is available. To access all media, simply go to **www.halleonard.com/mylibrary** and enter the code found on page 1 of this book. This will grant you instant access to every file. You can download to your computer, tablet, or phone, or stream the media live.

ABOUT THE AUTHOR

Sarah Jeffery is one of the world's foremost promoters of the recorder and a passionate champion of music education. She has been invited to perform and teach worldwide, and her popular YouTube channel *Team Recorder* delivers inspiring, accessible recorder content to over 200,000 subscribers. Sarah has featured across BBC radio and television and her debut album *Constellations* was released in 2018. She is Professor of Recorder at the Royal College of Music in London and Honorary Vice President of the UK's Society of Recorder Players.

This book is dedicated to her two greatest inspirations and cheerleaders, Jon and Bodil.

www.sarahjeffery.com

BASIC MUSICAL SYMBOLS

The language of music is written as notes on a **staff**. The staff consists of five lines, with four spaces between the lines. The location of each note on the staff determines its pitch (highness or lowness). The higher the note is placed on the staff, the higher it sounds. A note with a deeper pitch appears lower on the staff. At the beginning of the staff is a **clef** sign. For this recorder book, we use the treble clef.

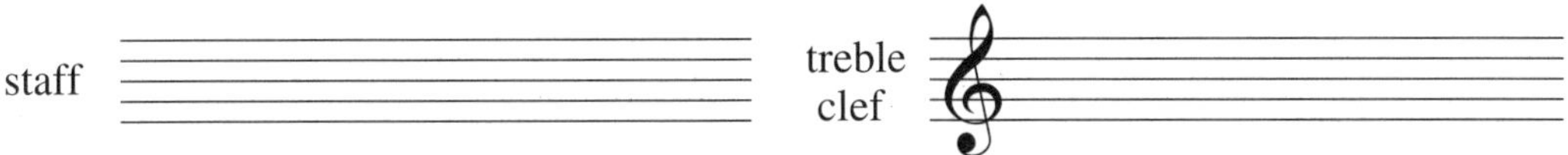

Notes that go above or below this staff range are placed on **ledger lines**.

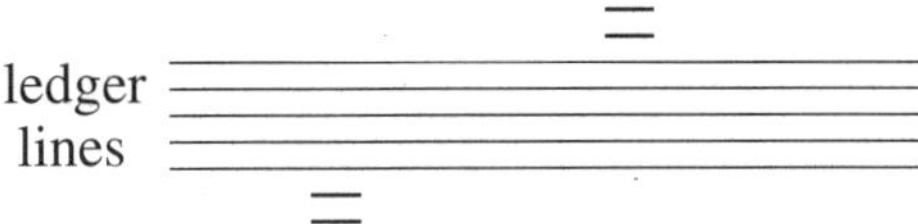

Each line and space has a letter name. The lines are, from bottom to top, E-G-B-D-F. This is easy to remember as "Every Good Boy Does Fine." The spaces are, from bottom to top, F-A-C-E.

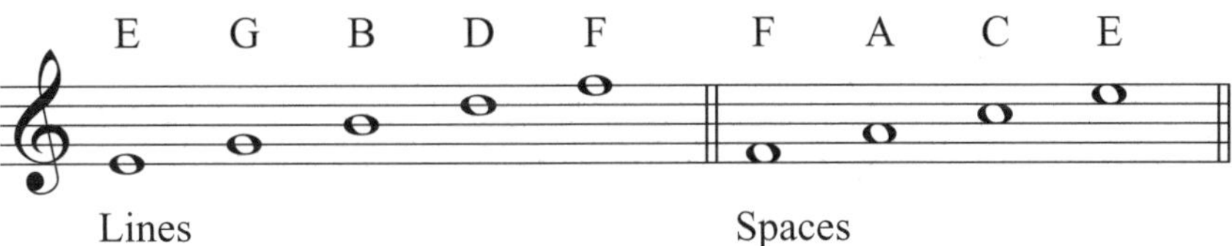

For this book, we'll only be encountering one note on a lower ledger line.

Music consists of notes or pitches that are set to a **beat**. The staff is divided by **bar lines** into units called **measures** or bars. A **double bar line** is used to indicate a transition, end of an extract (thin lines), or the end of a piece (thick end line).

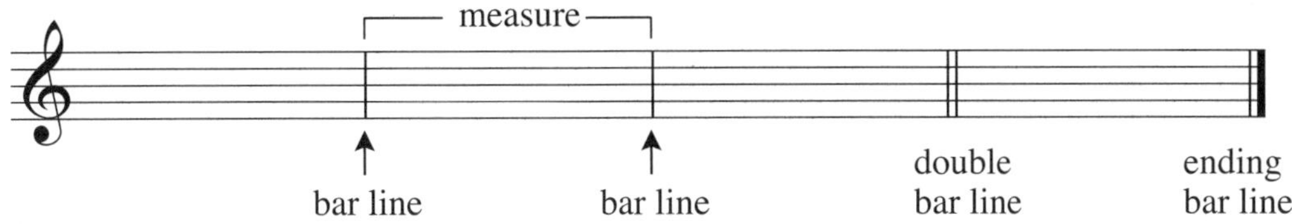

Each measure contains a specific number of beats. This is indicated by the **time signature**, which is typically located next to the clef at the beginning of a piece of music. It appears as two numbers. The top number indicates the number of beats in each measure. The bottom number tells us what kind of note gets one beat. You can remember this by asking "how many of what?" Here are some common time signatures:

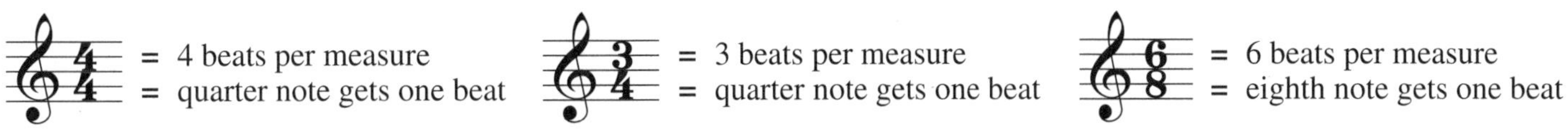

RHYTHM VALUES

Besides pitch, notes also indicate the duration, or how long the note lasts within a measure. Different types of notes have different durations.

NOTES

- whole note = 4 beats
- half note = 2 beats
- quarter note = 1 beat
- eighth note = 1/2 beat
- 16th note = 1/4 beat

REST VALUES

A rest, or the silence between the notes, also has a duration, just like the notes. Their corresponding values are listed below.

RESTS

- whole rest = 4 beats*
- half rest = 2 beats
- quarter rest = 1 beat
- eighth rest = 1/2 beat
- 16th rest = 1/4 beat

* This is also the symbol for an entire measure of silence in any time signature.

YOUR RECORDER

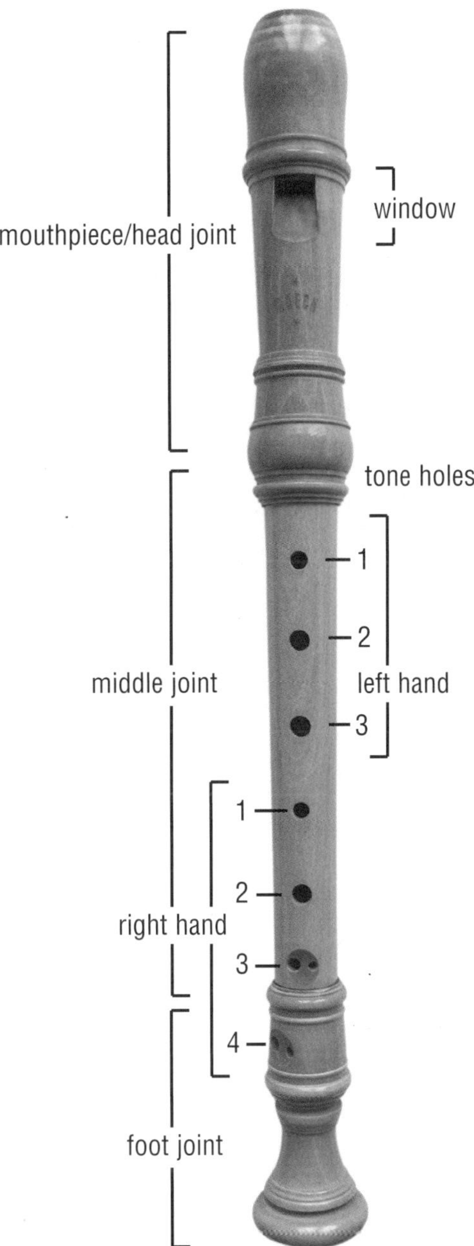

This picture is of a **soprano** (or **descant**) recorder. You can use the *Hal Leonard Recorder Method* with a soprano or tenor recorder in C.

CARING FOR YOUR RECORDER

Watch the video for expert guidance on looking after your instrument. To keep your recorder in good condition, it will be important to:

- Warm the head joint under your arm before you play, to prevent the formation of condensation.
- Wipe the instrument out with a cloth after playing.
- Let your recorder dry completely before packing away again.

 HOW TO HOLD YOUR RECORDER

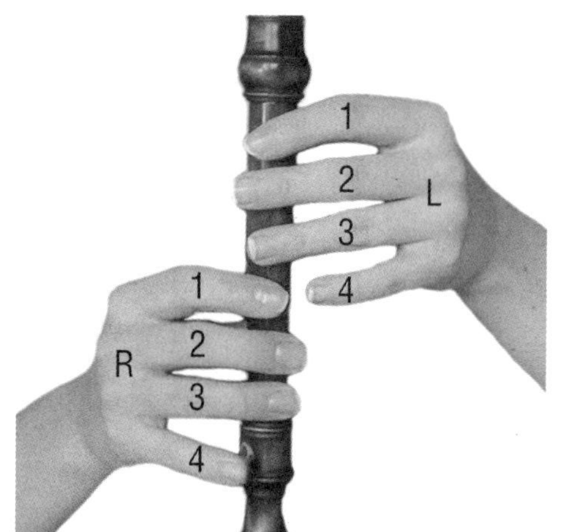

Watch the video and look at the pictures to help you. Hold your recorder out in front, placing your left hand near the top and your right hand towards the bottom.

- Press your left thumb over the hole underneath the recorder. Put your right thumb under the recorder, roughly opposite the fourth hole.
- We are looking for the most relaxed and natural posture. Stand/sit up straight and keep your shoulders at ease. Your elbows should float free and not be stuck to your sides.
- Hold the recorder at an angle around 45 degrees from your body; raising it up a little helps to balance the instrument.
- Try to find your most natural hand position. Make sure your wrists are not rotated sideways or dropped down.
- When holding the recorder, imagine you have a small apple in each hand.

HOW TO PRACTICE

You have this book packed full of great music, but how do you actually improve? Just playing the pieces over and over is not always the best way. In this video we will cover:

- How much should I be practicing?
- How do I know what to do?
- How can I identify trouble areas and solve them?
- How can I keep practice interesting?

INVENTING SOUNDS

Before we begin to play musical notes, let's explore having fun and making our own sounds on the recorder. Anything is possible! First, remove the head joint from the main body of the instrument. Then, watching the video, try making these sounds!

Once you've mastered making the sounds, play around with them in the following ways:

- Loud and soft
- Energetic and lazy.
- Repeating over and over.
- Linking different sounds together, one after another.

You can even devise a musical composition:

- Try writing a short story where moments can be represented by the sounds you've invented. Make it as funny as you like. Ask someone to read it out while you accompany with your sounds!
- If you are making music with a teacher or friend, could you have a conversation with these sounds? Are your characters chatting or arguing? Are you laughing together or interrupting each other angrily?
- Take your favorite sounds and devise a short piece based on them. Repeating the same sound at the beginning and the end of your piece will help. You can vary how loud or soft you play and the order that you link the sounds together. Record it on a device to reflect back on.

NOTES G AND E

NOTE G

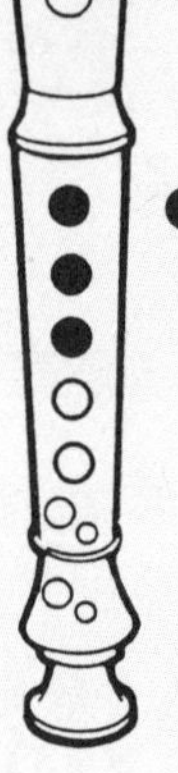

To play the note G:

- Place your left thumb over the hole underneath the recorder.
- Cover the top three holes nearest your mouth with your first, second, and third fingers.
- This is the fingering for the note G.
- To help hold the instrument, put your right thumb under the recorder opposite the fourth hole.

On the recorder, you begin every note with the tongue. Whisper a "doo" sound while blowing air through the recorder. This is known as **tonguing**.

It's important that you play the tunes in this book at a speed (**tempo**) that is comfortable. That's why specific metronome markings have been avoided. The performance indication above the staff is there to give you a general feel for the spirit and intent of the music. You can speed up or slow down the backing and demonstration audio to suit your needs, without impacting on pitch.

TONGUE EVERY NOTE

GO WITH THE FLOW

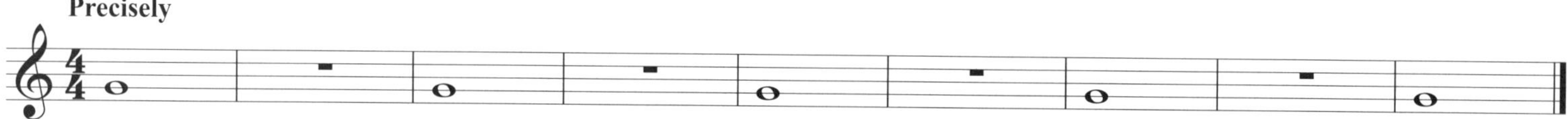

OVER TO YOU

Let's practice tonguing inventively. Play along with the video and try out your own rhythms on the note G. For this, you can use the backing track called "Improv on G."

GO LAZY

Chill

Seen at the start of the music, this is know as a **key signature**. At the moment, it doesn't impact the notes we are learning. We'll find out more about key signatures from page 41.

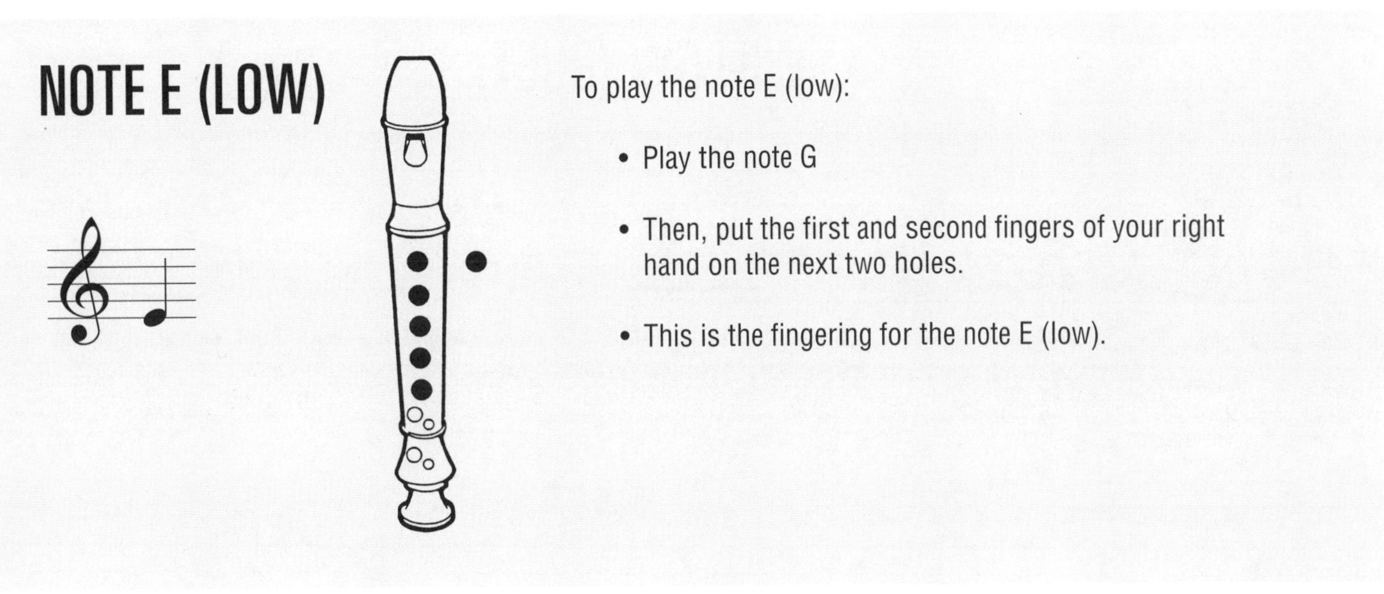

NOTE E (LOW)

To play the note E (low):

- Play the note G
- Then, put the first and second fingers of your right hand on the next two holes.
- This is the fingering for the note E (low).

THE BEAR DANCE

English Folk Tune

OVER TO YOU

Low notes like the E we have learned sound best when you blow with **warm air**, as if you were misting up a window. Watch the video to see how to get the best sounding E possible!

GENTLE DREAMS

Listen to the backing-track audio. Over the music, play long E notes in any rhythm of your choice. Try for a lovely, warm sound, applying what you've just learned in the "Over to You" video lesson. You can check out how to do this in the video lesson for this activity.

OVER TO YOU

A **duet** is a piece of music written for two players. There are two musical parts stacked on top of one another. For all the duets in this book, you should play the top staff. Your teacher can play the bottom staff. If you don't have a partner to play with, simply use the online teacher demonstration track.

WILLOW (DUET)

CHEESE AND PICKLE (DUET)

NOTES G AND E TOGETHER

OVER TO YOU

Check out the video lesson and learn how to combine your very first two notes together in a stress-free and musical way!

,

This symbol is called a **comma**, or "breath mark." It tells you where to take a breath. Breathe in through your mouth, not your nose!

WHOLESOME NOTES

This semicircle with a dot is called a **fermata**. It tells you to hold the note for a little longer than its value.

KNIGHT'S TALE

OVER TO YOU

Ask your teacher to play the piece "Toad in a Mole Hole" or access the online audio track. The notes G and E fit with this tune.

1. Play along on G and/or E, playing whole notes. (Count four beats on each note.)
2. Play along on G and/or E, playing half notes. (Count two beats on each note.)
3. Play along on G and/or E, tonguing your own rhythms.

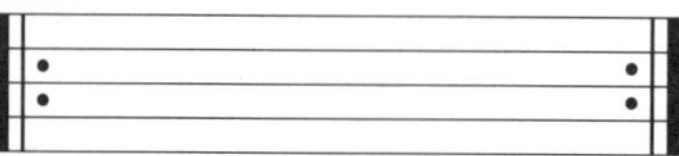

These are **repeat bar lines**. Music that lies between these two symbols should be repeated once through again. If there is no forward-facing repeat sign, go back to the beginning of the music.

TOAD IN A MOLE HOLE (IN C)

FOR THE TEACHER

HOP TO IT

ON THE COUNT (DUET)

Swung

MUSICAL CLOCK

NOTE A

NOTE A

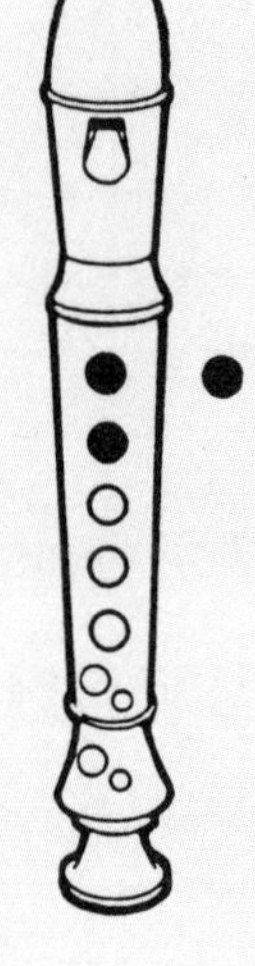

To play the note A:

- Play the note G.
- Then, take off your left-hand third finger. You are now covering just two holes with your left hand.
- This is the fingering for the note A.

SUNRISE, SUNSET

Warm

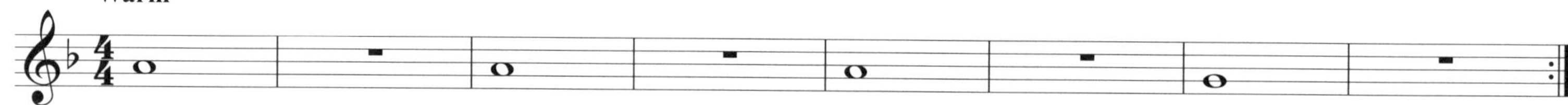

TROUBADOUR

With confidence

COUNTING IN THREE

We are about to count in three for the first time. Read below and watch the video to see how to do this easily.

Counting in three involves reading **dotted notes**. We'll begin with the dotted-half note. A dot next to a notehead adds half of the beat value. A regular half note has two beats and the dot adds one more beat, so a dotted-half note is held for three beats.

A dot adds half the value of the note.

2 Beats + 1 Beat = 3 Beats

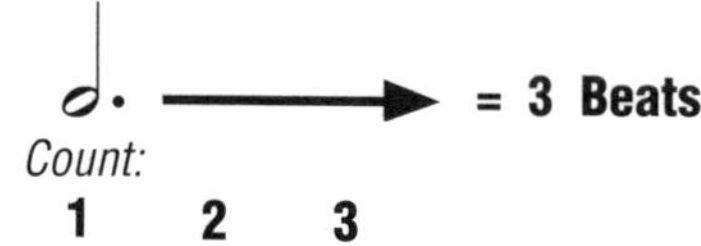

On this page, we are playing in 3/4 time. You'll notice the following exercise has a 3/4 time signature. Since there are three beats per measure, this rhythm works well and is easy to count.

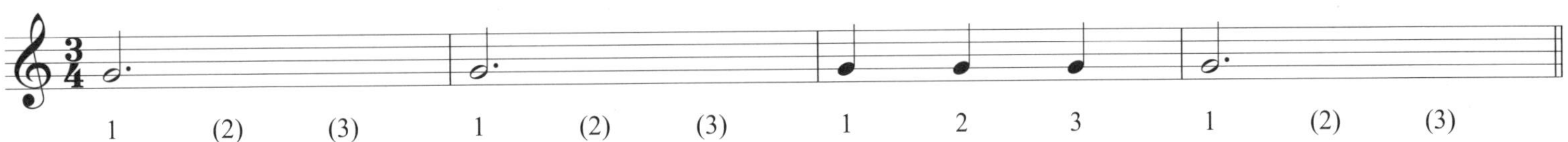

WALTZ

NORTHERN LIGHTS

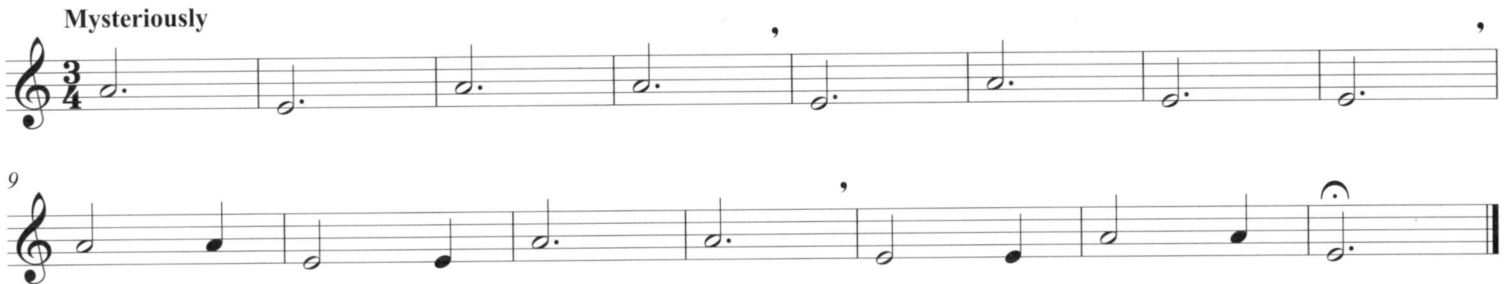

SILVER STARS

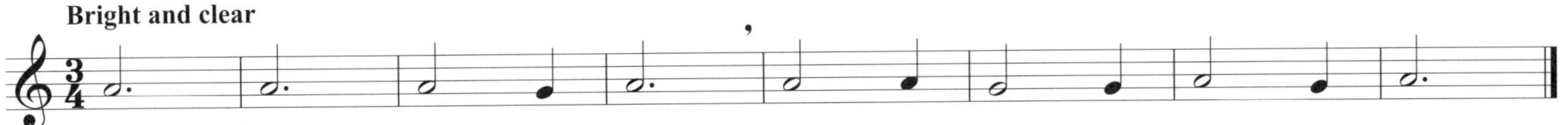

Notice the breath mark at the end of measure 4. Any time you need to remember to take a breath, circle the relevant breath mark on your music or write this symbol as a reminder. Use a pencil with an eraser, since where you breathe may alter depending on how fast you play.

OVER TO YOU

Listen to the backing track for "Northern Lights" on page 15. Can you hear the sense of three beats in a measure?

1. Try playing along with dotted-half notes (worth three beats), choosing between the notes G, E, or A. Sometimes it will fit, other times it will clash. That's fine! Keep to the steady beat, counting "one-two-three."
2. On the note A, try tonguing your own rhythm along with the backing track. You can choose long note values or split the beat up into shorter values. Concentrate on keeping to the beat.

Try playing dotted-half notes again in **common time**, a time signature that is another name for 4/4. It is notated with a large "C."

Each measure gets four beats. Be sure to count along, either by tapping your foot or with the help of a metronome. Make certain the dotted-half note is held for three full beats before you play the quarter note.

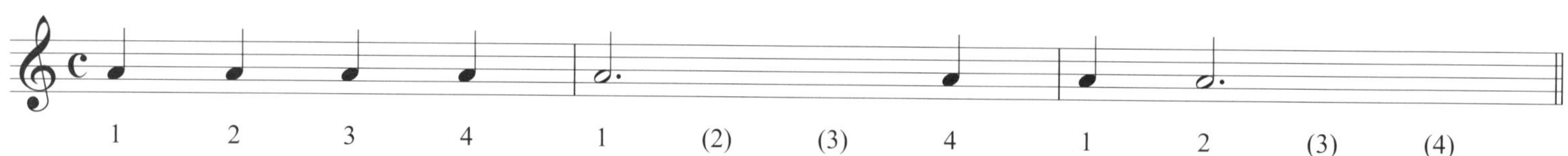

NOTES G, E, AND A TOGETHER

This is called a **pickup**. It is sometimes also known as an **upbeat** or an **anacrusis**. A **pickup** is a note or group of notes that stand on their own at the beginning of a tune before the first full measure. The word "happy" in the "Happy Birthday" song is a pickup!

IT'S RAINING, IT'S POURING

We subtract the length of the pickup from the final measure. That's why there are only two beats, here!

SPRING (DUET)

from THE FOUR SEASONS

Antonio Vivaldi

Joyfully

CLOUDS

As you play "Clouds," listen to the backing audio. Try to hear how your line interacts with the chords. Sometimes it clashes, sometimes it fits.

OVER TO YOU

Now, try playing "Clouds" again with a difference!

1. First, play the whole thing along with the backing track but only using the G note or an A note. How does that change the feeling of the music?
2. Finally, play it again but this time moving freely between E, G, and A. See if you can make your own version of the piece that you enjoy!

CUCKOO

This bowed line is called a **tie**. A tie joins two notes of the same pitch together. You hold the note for the combined value!

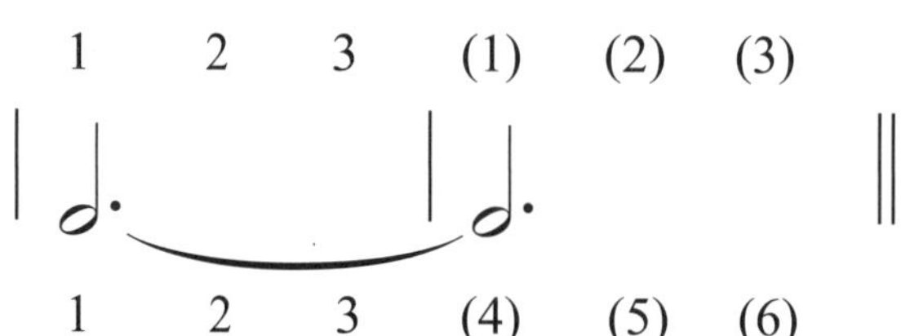

WHISPERING WHIRLWIND

When two notes are joined by lines like this, you move between them at a fast speed for their full duration. This is known as **tremolo**. Listen to the demonstration audio to get an idea. You can also practice this technique in the video lesson from page 17.

ROLLING IN THE DEEP

Words and Music by Adele Adkins
and Paul Epworth

OVER TO YOU

The tied rhythms in Adele's "Rolling in the Deep" can be tricky to count. Listen to the demo recording to get comfortable. Then, play it once more with the backing track but fill in the last three measures yourself with G, E, or A. Try different versions until you hear one that you like!

NOTE B

NOTE B

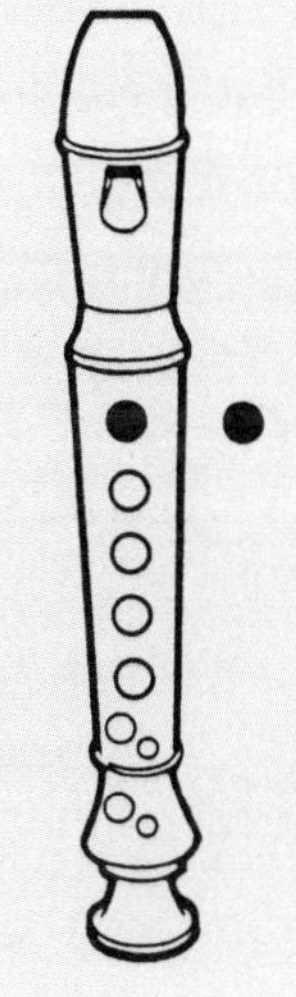

To play the note B:

- Play the note A.
- Then, take off your left-hand second finger. You are now covering just one hole with your left hand.
- This is the fingering for the note B.

CITY LIGHTS

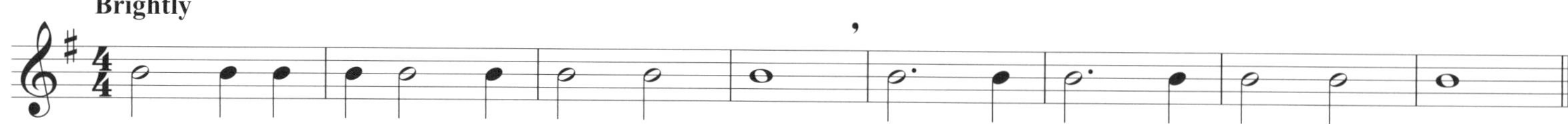

BY THE BROOK

AU CLAIR DE LA LUNE

French Folksong

COUNTING EIGHTH NOTES

Watch the video lesson to know how to play eighth notes with confidence. We count eighth notes like this:

Each individual eighth note = 1/2 a beat.

Two eighth notes = 1 beat. When counting eighth notes, it can help to say "and" (&) between each beat.

Two or more eighth notes are joined by a horizontal line called a **beam**.

HOT CROSS BUNS

Traditional

TAKE A LITTLE SUNSHINE (DUET)

OVER TO YOU

Go back to "Tongue Every Note" on page 8. Try playing the whole piece again but using eight eighth notes in every measure instead of four quarter notes.

BLUE SONG

RADIO GA GA

Moderately

Words and Music by Roger Taylor

HEY YA!

Bright rock

Words and Music by Andre Benjamin

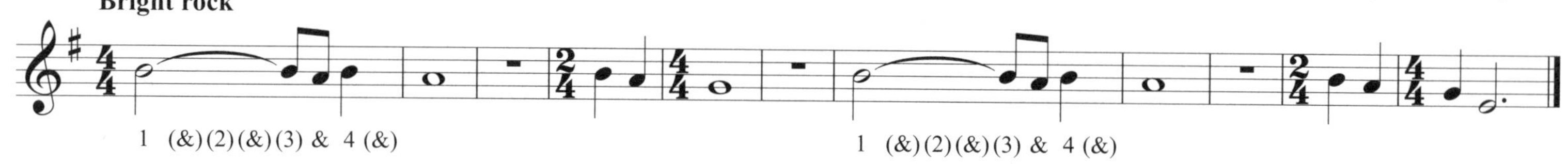

BREATHING 101

Breathing and blowing are the most important aspects of playing the recorder well and comfortably. Watch the video to ensure you breathe and blow in the best way!

BREATHING IN

- Breathe in through your mouth, **not your nose**!
- Keep your throat, neck, and shoulders relaxed.
- Imagine the air going down into the bottom of your belly.

You should be able to take in adequate air when you reach a breath mark. Remember to start your next note on time. For example, you can cut a long note slightly short to give yourself enough time to breath in before you go on.

BLOWING OUT

- Imagine a steady stream of air, like blowing up a balloon.
- You don't have to stop and start the air for every note.
- Rather than letting the air go, imagine it streaming out gradually like a continuous ribbon.
- Don't be afraid to blow! The air into a recorder is like fuel for a car: you need enough to make it go.

HELP! MY SOUND IS WOBBLY

Without your recorder, practice blowing out a long stream of air on the syllable "fff." This creates resistance, which will make it easier to hold a stable tone.

HELP! I'M RUNNING OUT OF AIR

- Warming up with a few long notes every day trains your stamina.
- Check you're not breathing out through your nose as you play.
- Make sure you breathe in the same place each time you play a particular piece. This develops muscle memory, helping you to remember how much air to breathe in.
- If you feel "stuck," then stop and put down your recorder. Next, take a big breath in and out to relax and reset.

NOTE D (LOW)

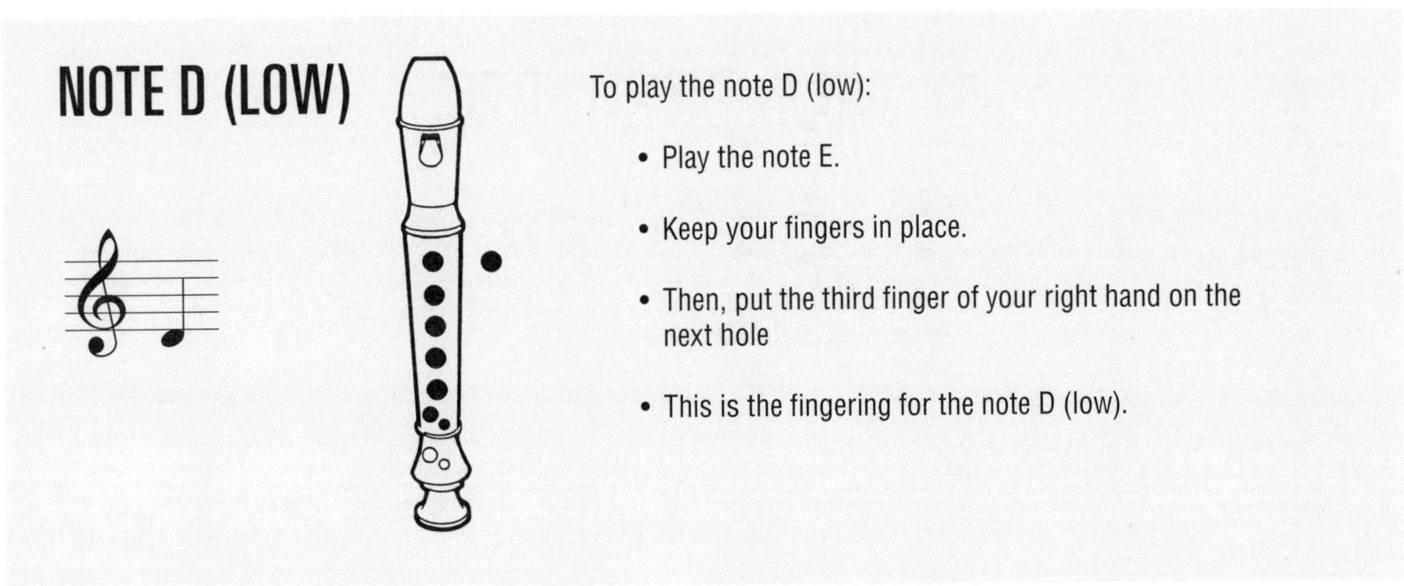

To play the note D (low):

- Play the note E.
- Keep your fingers in place.
- Then, put the third finger of your right hand on the next hole
- This is the fingering for the note D (low).

WAVES

This rest symbol indicates two measures (or eight beats) of silence.

CHATTER WITH THE ANGELS

Traditional Sacred

Busy, with hope

DOWNTON ABBEY (THEME)

from DOWNTON ABBEY

Music by John Lunn

A **canon** is a musical composition in which two or more people play the same melody, starting at different moments.

This canon, "Cat in the Plumtree," can be played with up to four players! "Player 1" starts. "Player 2" enters once "Player 1" has reached figure 2. If you don't have a teacher or another player to perform with you, play along with the backing track.

CAT IN THE PLUMTREE

LEGATO AND SLURS

Until now, we have started every note with the tongue. We can also play without the tongue when we want notes to be smoothly connected. This is known as playing **legato.** On sheet music, a bowed line connecting notes of different pitches indicates when to play legato. This line is known as a **slur**. If you see two or more notes joined by a slur, it means that you tongue only the first in the group. Check out the video lesson to fully understand how to apply this.

LEGATISSIMO

O, BRIGHT MORNING

Gently

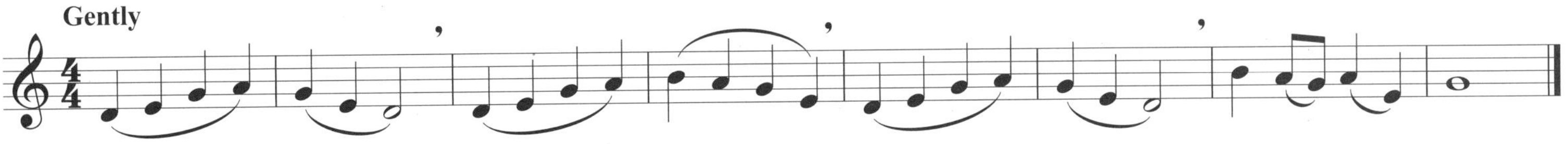

BOFFONS (DUET)

Jacob van Eyck

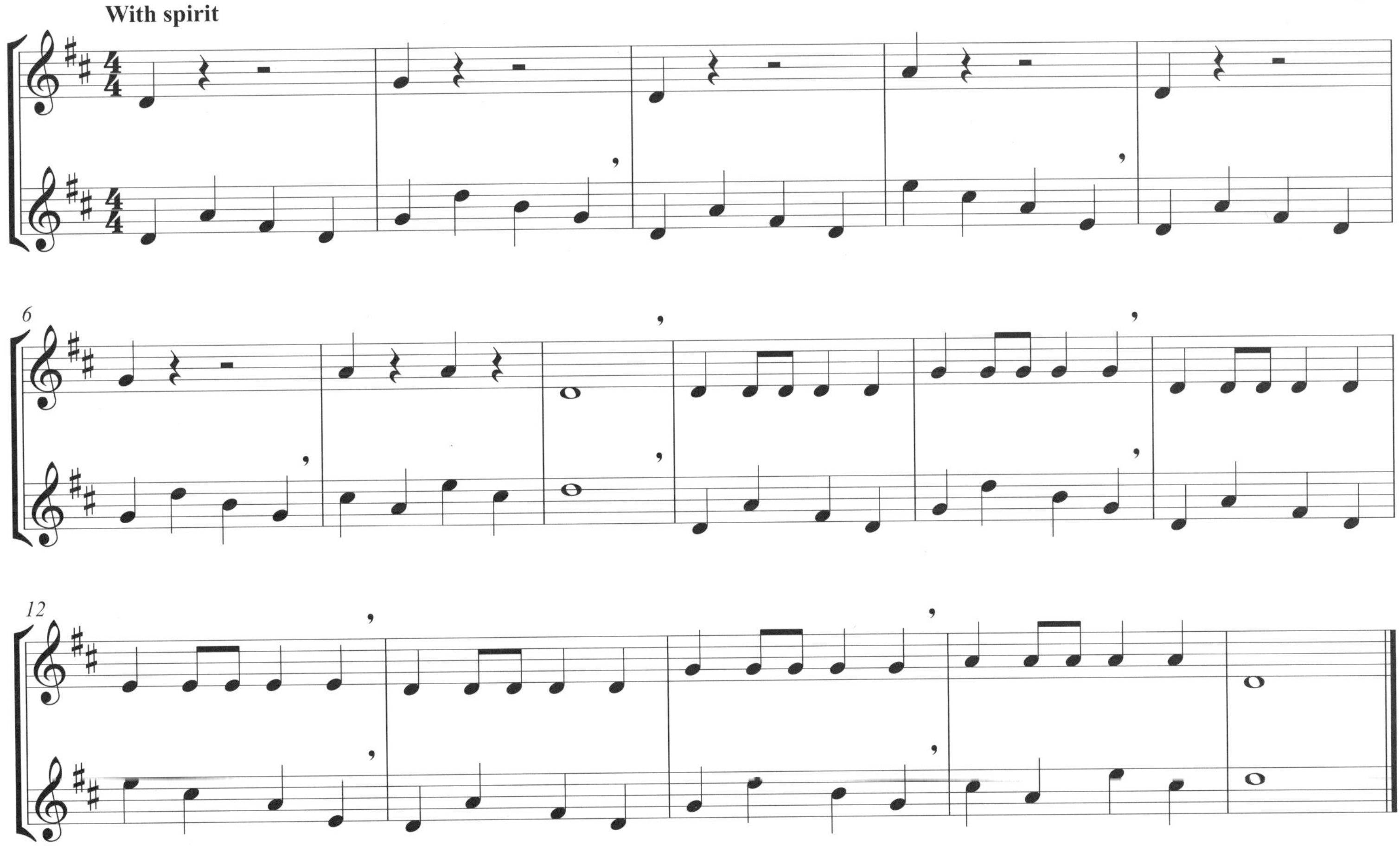
With spirit
6
12

OVER TO YOU

Put on the backing track "Gentle Dreams" from page 9. Play along with any combination of D, E, and G notes in a legato phrase. (Tongue the first note and slur the rest, following wherever your fingers take you.)

NOTE C (HIGH)

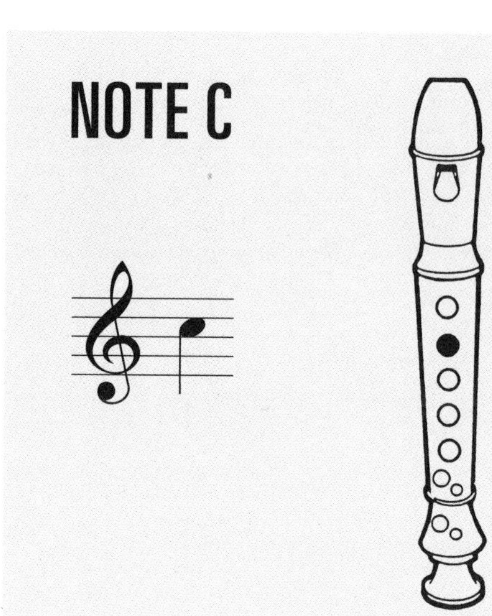

To play the note C (high):

- Play the note A.
- Then, remove your left first finger.
- Keep your second finger and thumb covering the holes.
- This is the fingering for the note C (high).

RAIN, RAIN GO AWAY

HALLELUJAH CHORUS

STACCATO PLAYING

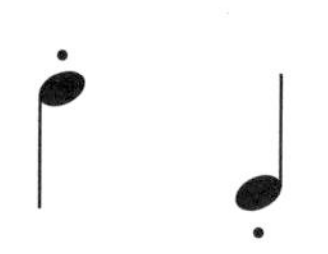

Staccato means to play a note short and spiky. We do this by stopping the sound with our tongue. You can tell when to play a note staccato because you'll see a dot above or below the notehead. The video lesson will help you master this.

MINUET IN G (DUET)

Christian Petzold

QUESTA DOLCE SIRENA

Jacob van Eyck
from Music by Giovanni Gastoldi

DOTTED-QUARTER NOTE

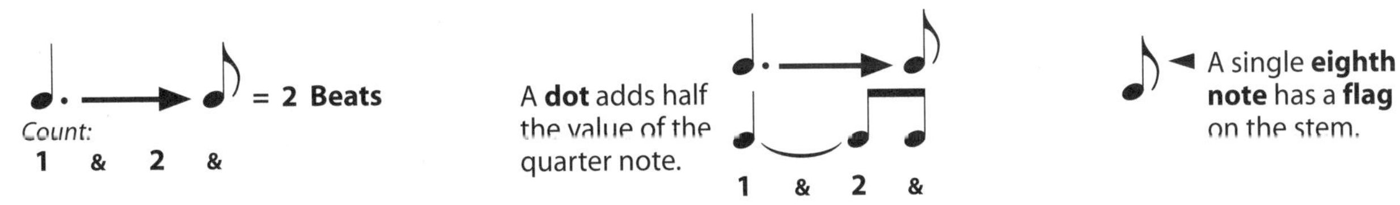

You'll find some guidance on playing this rhythm in the video lesson for our new high C note.

KAS A-BAHR

Traditional Breton Folk Dance

YESTERDAY

Words and Music by John Lennon
and Paul McCartney

Lyrically

FIRST AND SECOND ENDINGS

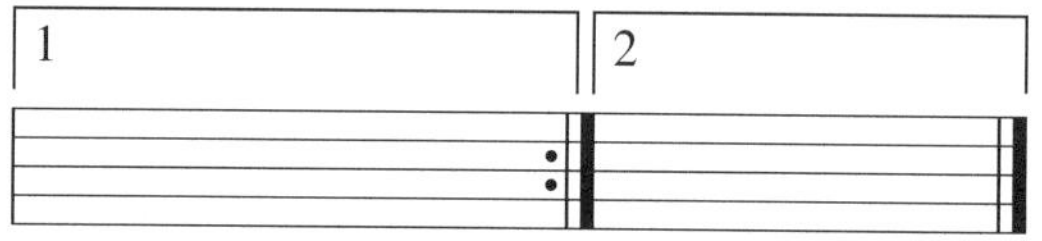

Play your music up to and including the first ending measure(s). Then, repeat from the start of the piece. On the repeat, skip the first ending and play the second-ending measure(s) instead.

OPUS ONE

Words and Music by Sy Oliver

Moderate Jump tempo

Although there are regular eighth notes printed in "Opus One," you'll hear it sounds much more like the original tune if we play each pair with a loose, "long-short" feel. These are called **swing eighths**. Have a listen to the backing and demonstration audio to hear how this is done!

SEPTEMBER

Words and Music by Maurice White,
Al McKay and Allee Willis

Moderate Rock

AUTUMN EVE

OVER TO YOU

Practicing staccato is not only good for your tongue; it's great for improving your sense of rhythm, too. Take a piece you know already and try playing it all staccato, including the long notes. Now, go back to "Questa Dolce Sirena" on page 27. Try moving the staccato dots onto different notes and listen to how that changes the feeling of the music. Experiment!

TONGUING 101

Beginning every note with the tongue gives your music definition and can be a great tool for creating musical expression. The extent to which we play notes smoothly or detached is known as **articulation.** The video lesson applies this concept practically.

WHERE SHOULD I TONGUE?

Try to find the cleanest, most efficient movement possible. Only the tip of the tongue should be moving, and it should strike the gummy ridge **behind** your teeth, not on your teeth.

You can use a "t" or a "d" sound. The "t" is stronger and the "d" more subtle. Performers often mix the two syllables to create expressive contrast in the music.

HOW CAN I USE ARTICULATION IN MY PLAYING?

Articulation on the recorder is like speaking or singing. Watch the video lesson to see how different types of articulation can transform your playing. In it, you'll discover there are different colors of articulation between the opposite ends of staccato and legato:

Staccato

We've met this already on page 26. Notes that have a dot above or below the notehead are to be played short and spiky, stopping the note with the tongue.

Detached

This involves leaving a little space between notes, so they remain separated but not spiky staccato! There is no special notation for this articulation.

Portato
Like singing "la, la, la" in one breath. In the video lesson, this articulation is referred to as "smooth."

Legato

We've met this already on page 24. Notes grouped within a slur are to be played smoothly, without the tongue.

Ideas to try:

- Choose a piece of music and play all the notes staccato or legato.
- Choose two notes and alternate playing one legato for four beats and the other staccato. Or make up a staccato/legato pattern using the notes.
- Think of a mood (e.g., relaxed, energetic, aggressive) and try to express it through articulation.
- Sing a phrase first, then try to copy what you did on the recorder.
- Look at the articulation for a piece of music and play the opposite!

The different types of articulation notated in this book are just intended as suggestions. You are free to experiment and interpret your own articulation within pieces. If you play something you like, keep it!

NOTE D (HIGH)

NOTE D

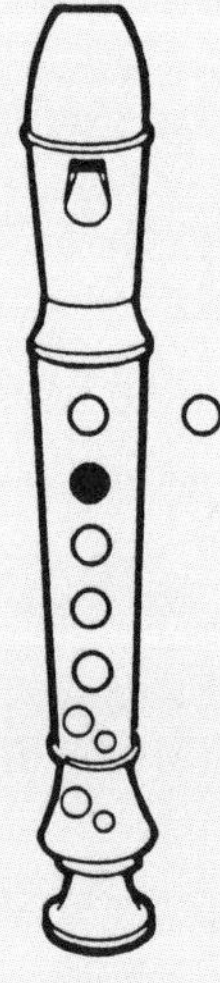

To play the note D (high):

- Play the note C (high).
- Now, take your thumb off the back hole.
- This is the fingering for the note D (high).

IN THE BALANCE (DUET)

Balancing the recorder can be tricky when playing the high D, as you take your thumb away. Being prepared for this can make a big difference! If you are still feeling wobbly, try raising the recorder a little so it can rest more securely on your thumb.

SUPER TROUPER

Words and Music by Benny Andersson
and Bjorn Ulvaeus

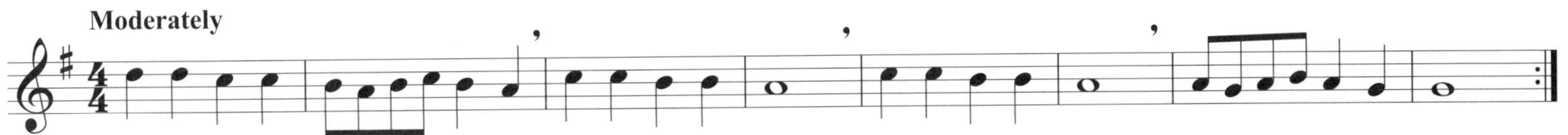

NEW WORLD SYMPHONY (THEME)

Antonín Dvořák

RHYTHM 101

Here are some tips and tricks for figuring out the rhythms in your music. You can refer back to the rhythmic summary on page 4 for reference, too! The methods below build on different learning styles. Combine them together in a way that works best for you.

BY EAR

The adage goes, "If you can sing it, you can play it." If you know how the rhythm is supposed to sound, you are most of the way there! Look at the sheet music again for "Rain, Rain, Go Away." It's a familiar tune. Listen to the audio and read the music through, matching your knowledge of the tune to the rhythmic notation on the staff. Singing along helps, too. You will gradually come to recognize familiar rhythmic patterns when they reappear in a new piece.

BEAT IT

This relies on feeling and identifying the beat in your music. Look at where the notes in your piece match up with the beats per measure. Are they on or off the beat (**syncopated**)? Using the beat as a basis will help your music come alive.

BREAK IT DOWN

Subdivide the rhythms of your piece into their smallest note value, such as eighth notes. Then count throughout in that note value, ensuring you understand how long the notes should be in relation to one another. Do this for small passages of music and, as you get confident, gradually start linking everything together. This is especially helpful for tied notes, dotted notes, and syncopation.

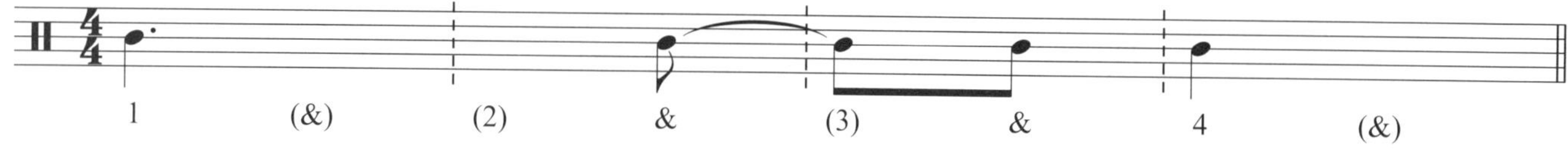

ADD LYRICS

Assigning words to rhythmic sections can make a world of difference! Try the following simple example:

MY LORD DELIVERED DANIEL

Samuel Coleridge-Taylor

Need help with the rhythm for this piece? The video lesson for RHYTHM 101 on page 32 will be helpful. You can also listen to the demo audio and copy what you hear!

A MORNING SUNBEAM (DUET)

from THREE SKETCHES FOR LITTLE PIANISTS

Florence Price

WAITING ON A MIRACLE

from ENCANTO

Music and Lyrics by Lin-Manuel Miranda

MAZURKA

Traditional Mazurka

OVER TO YOU

Making mistakes when practicing is an essential part of learning. If you play everything perfectly the first time, you won't have learned anything! Watch the video lesson. Then, choose a piece you know well from this book and attempt to:

- Play the rhythm correctly, but with all different notes.
- Play it from back to front, starting with the very last note.
- Play the correct notes but inventing new rhythms.

SINGLE LADIES (PUT A RING ON IT)

Words and Music by Beyoncé Knowles,
Thaddis Harrell, Christopher Stewart and Terius Nash

In 6/4, there are six quarter-note beats in a measure. Here, beats 1 and 4 are the strong beats that will require a little extra emphasis. The exercise below shows the beat count for a three-measure rhythm in 6/4. Clap and count along to help you with the piece by Byrd. Parts of the beat count in parentheses are silent (i.e., you don't clap on them).

LA VOLTA

William Byrd

It can help to count this next song in eighth notes. Listen to the demo audio to get a feel for how the rhythm goes. The backing track will also be useful as it also contains the tune. We even learn this rhythm in the video lesson for RHYTHM 101 on page 32, so check that out too.

CAN YOU FEEL THE LOVE TONIGHT

from THE LION KING

Music by Elton John
Lyrics by Tim Rice

NOTE F

NOTE F

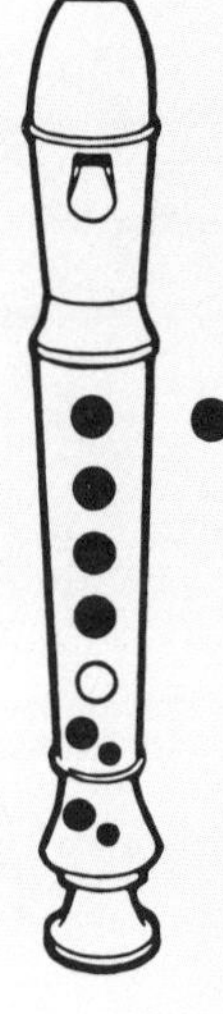

To play the note F:

- Play the note D (low).
- Add your right-hand pinky finger. Cover both small holes at the same time.
- Now, take off the second finger of your right hand.
- This is the fingering for the note F.

FREEFALL

JOLENE

Words and Music by Dolly Parton

EDELWEISS
from THE SOUND OF MUSIC

Lyrics by Oscar Hammerstein II
Music by Richard Rodgers

6/8 TIME

In 6/8 time, there are six eighth notes per measure. This is the same number of eighth notes as in a measure of 3/4. But in 6/8, the six eighth notes are organized into two groups of three. So we count, "One-and-ah, two-and-ah."

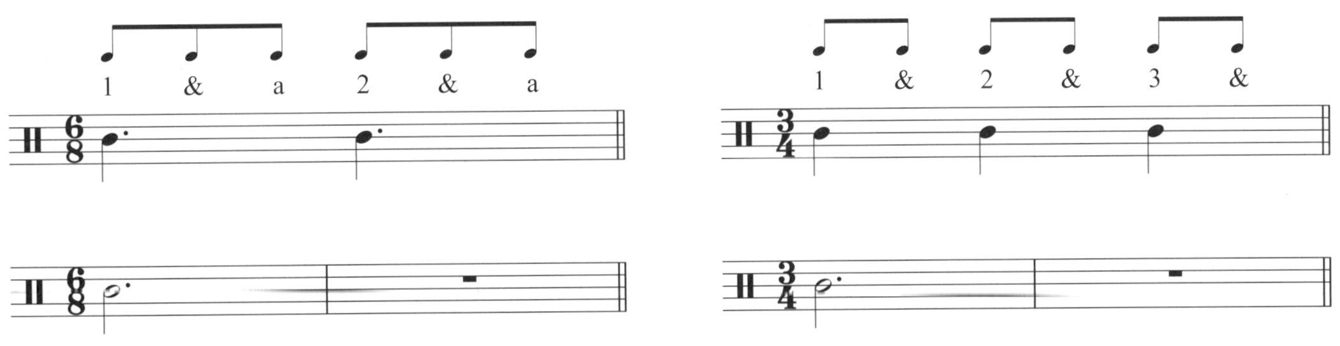

GREEN'S GROUND

PASE EL AGOA, MA JULIETA

Traditional

BRIGHT EYES (DUET)

from THREE SKETCHES FOR LITTLE PIANISTS

Florence Price

JEFF'S JIG

GREENSLEEVES

Sixteenth Century Traditional English

OVER TO YOU

For "Greensleeves," allegedly written by King Henry VIII, have a go at composing your own tune around the main melody, written on the small staff. Try out some ideas and write them in pencil on the main staff, underneath the melody. Use the backing track to experiment with what notes you want to use for your accompanying tune. Then, play the melody back using the online backing track. (Or, even better, with a teacher or recorder partner!) Make any amendments you wish to your melody on the staff using an eraser.

Composition exercises like this can be wonderful ways of connecting your recorder technique to aural skills and general musicianship. Before you get started, watch the video lesson on this to get guidance and inspiration!

OVERTURE
from L'AMANT ANONYME

Joseph Bologne

NOTE F#

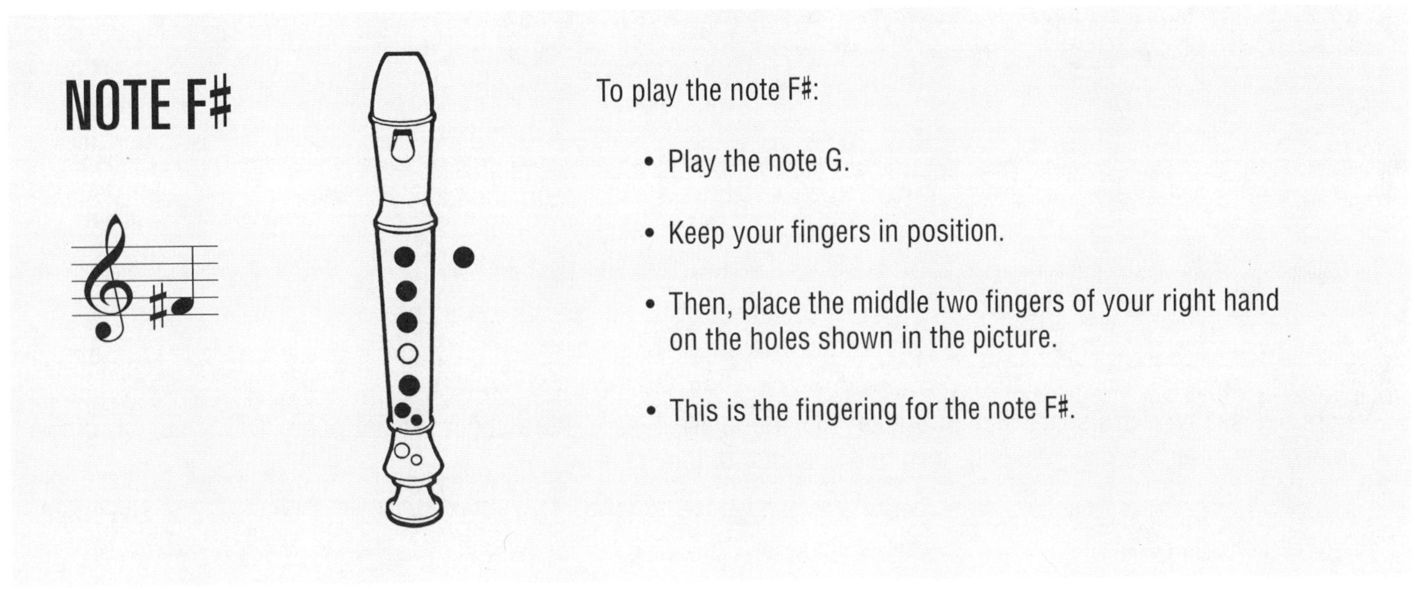

THE SHARP SIGN

This is a sharp sign. It raises a note's pitch by a half step. If you spot a sharp sign before the F note, it means you should play F#. You can see this in action during "The Bear's Pavane." When a note is sharpened, it stays that way throughout the entire measure.

THE BEAR'S PAVANE

You might also see the F# sign written as a **key signature** at the very beginning of a piece of music. This means whenever you see an F note in the music, you should play an F#. Even though the sign is on the top F line, it applies to any F on the staff.

READING'S GROUND

LI'L LIZA JANE

Words and Music by Countess Ada de Lachau

Here, we see an extra sharp sign in the key signature. We'll learn more about it from page 70. For now, it doesn't impact the notes we play. We only need to be mindful of the F♯.

SPRING

from THE FOUR SEASONS

Antonio Vivaldi

DAISY BELL (A BICYCLE BUILT FOR TWO)

Words and Music by Harry Dacre

LET IT GO

from FROZEN

Music and Lyrics by Kristen Anderson-Lopez
and Robert Lopez

EINE KLEINE NACHTMUSIK (DUET)

FIRST MOVEMENT

Wolfgang Amadeus Mozart

Lively

5

8

From now on, you might see some additional directions in the music:

- **Fine** = The end.
- **D.S. al Fine** = Go back to the 𝄋 sign and play until you reach "Fine."
- **D.C. al Fine** = Go back to the beginning and play until you reach "Fine."

THE BEAR DANCE

English Folk Tune

Always moving
6
11

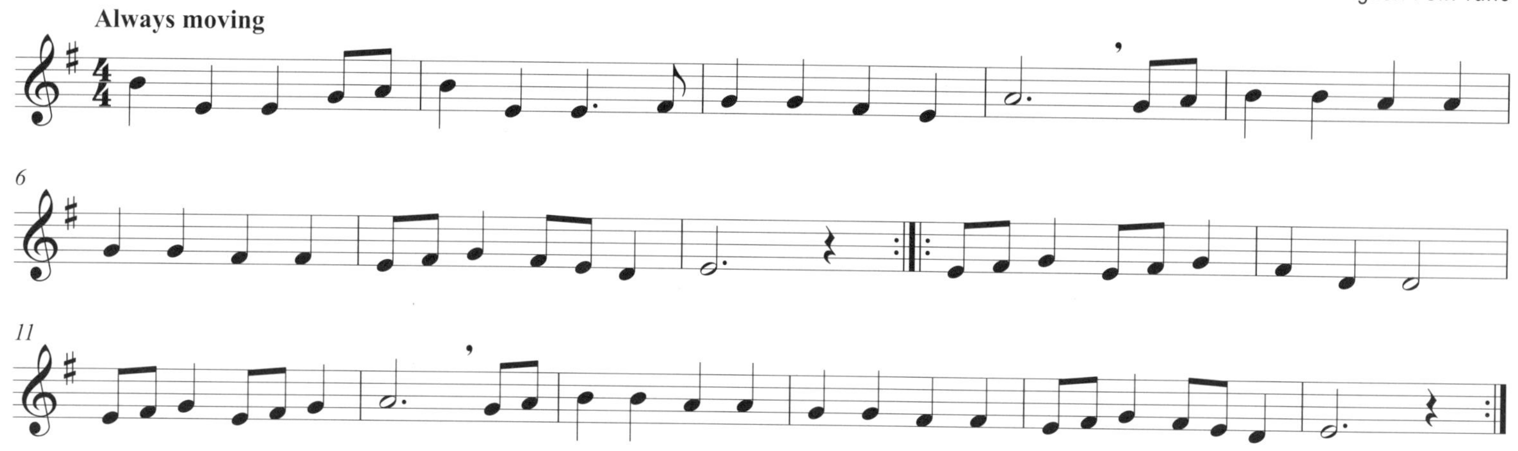

Back on page 9, you played an arrangement of this piece where the tune was in the backing track and the recorder part was just on the note E. Look how far you have come!

♮ THE NATURAL SIGN

This is a natural sign. Collectively, sharp and natural signs are known as **accidentals**. A natural sign cancels out any previous accidental. In "The Arrival," the key signature changes at measure 9; all F# notes in the piece become normal F notes. (You'll notice the natural sign is written on the high F note, the top staff line. The direction is universal so it applies to all F notes, whatever the pitch.)

THE ARRIVAL (DUET)

Francis Johnson

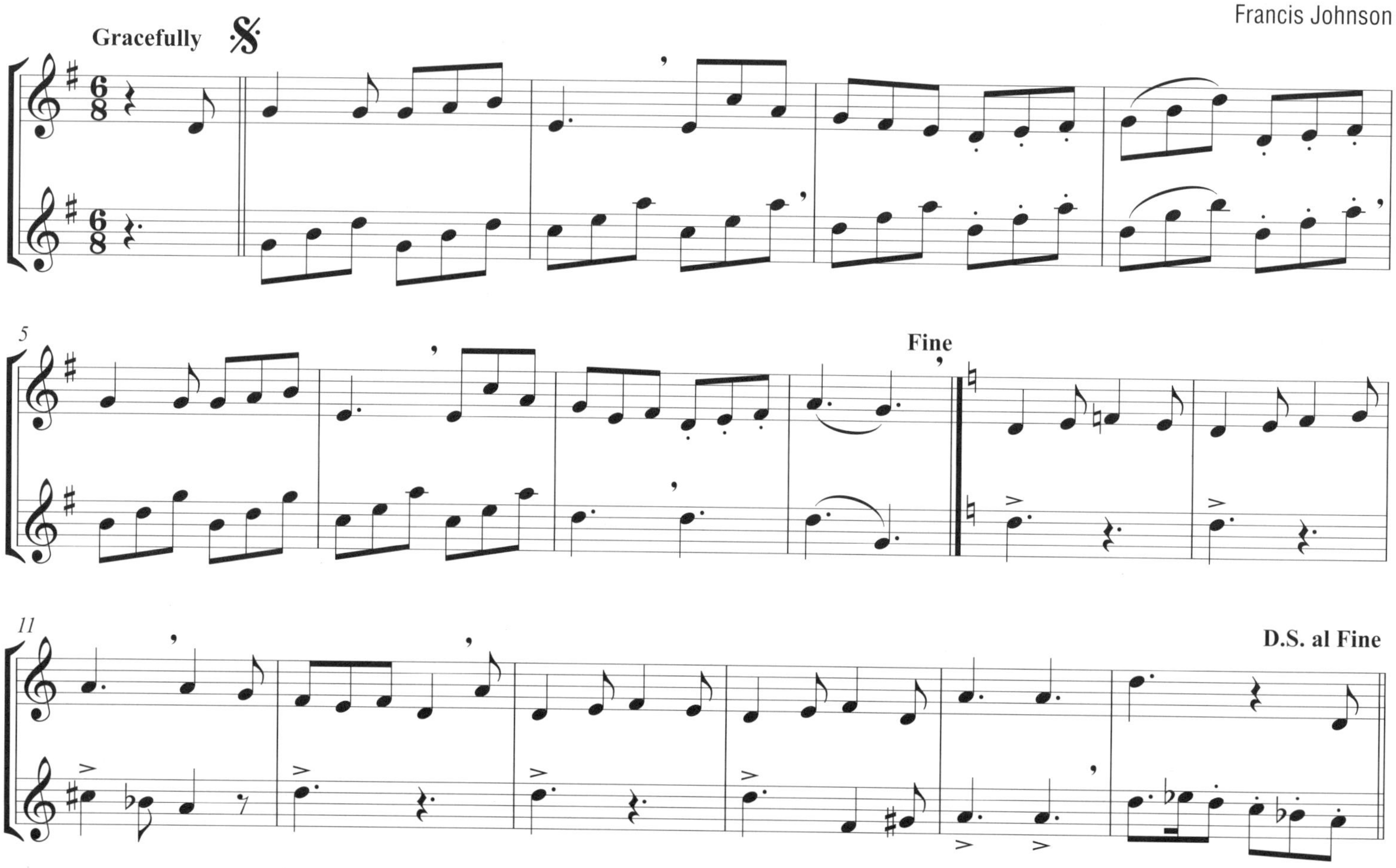
Gracefully
5
Fine
11
D.S. al Fine

YELLOW SUBMARINE

Words and Music by John Lennon
and Paul McCartney

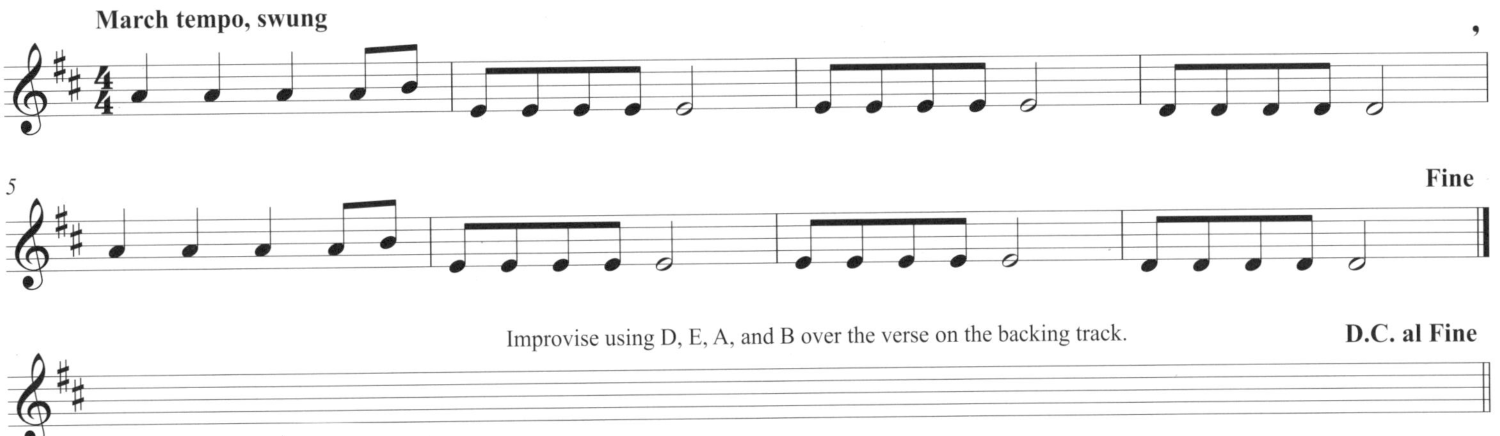

Although there are regular eighth notes printed in "Yellow Submarine," you'll hear it sounds much more like the original song if we play each pair with a loose, "long-short" feel. These are called **swing eighths**. Have a listen to the backing and demonstration audio to hear how this is done!

FINAL COUNTDOWN

Words and Music by Joey Tempest

PAVANE (LA BATAILLE)

Tielman Susato

CONCERT PROGRAM

The next four pieces comprise a spread of contemporary art music, classical favorites, and popular Disney. Together, they'll make for a lovely, short recital program that you could perform for friends or family along with the backing audio. What a beautiful way to celebrate your recorder journey so far!

CHANSON DE MA PATRIE

for Milan Pavan

Althea Talbot-Howard

- **Ritardando** (or **rit.**) = Gradually get slower.
- **A tempo** = Go back to the original speed (tempo).

PAPAGENO'S ARIA

from DIE ZAUBERFLÖTE

Wolfgang Amadeus Mozart

OVER TO YOU

Try recording yourself playing: a simple phone recording is fine. Give it a few days, then listen back. What do you like about your playing? (Compliments are important!) Can you identify one thing you'd like to work on in your next practice session? Save this recording for later.

In this fun piece, we are counting six quarter-note beats in each measure, with a little emphasis on beats 1 and 4. If you choose to have a go with the backing track, you'll notice that it has quite a groove and works against the rhythms of your tune. Make use of the facility to slow the audio down to a manageable speed, at first. You might even like to sing your melody over the top before attempting to play it. The demonstration audio will help you, too.

THE FAIRIE-ROUND

Anthony Holborne

PART OF YOUR WORLD
from THE LITTLE MERMAID

Music by Alan Menken
Lyrics by Howard Ashman

NOTE C (LOW)

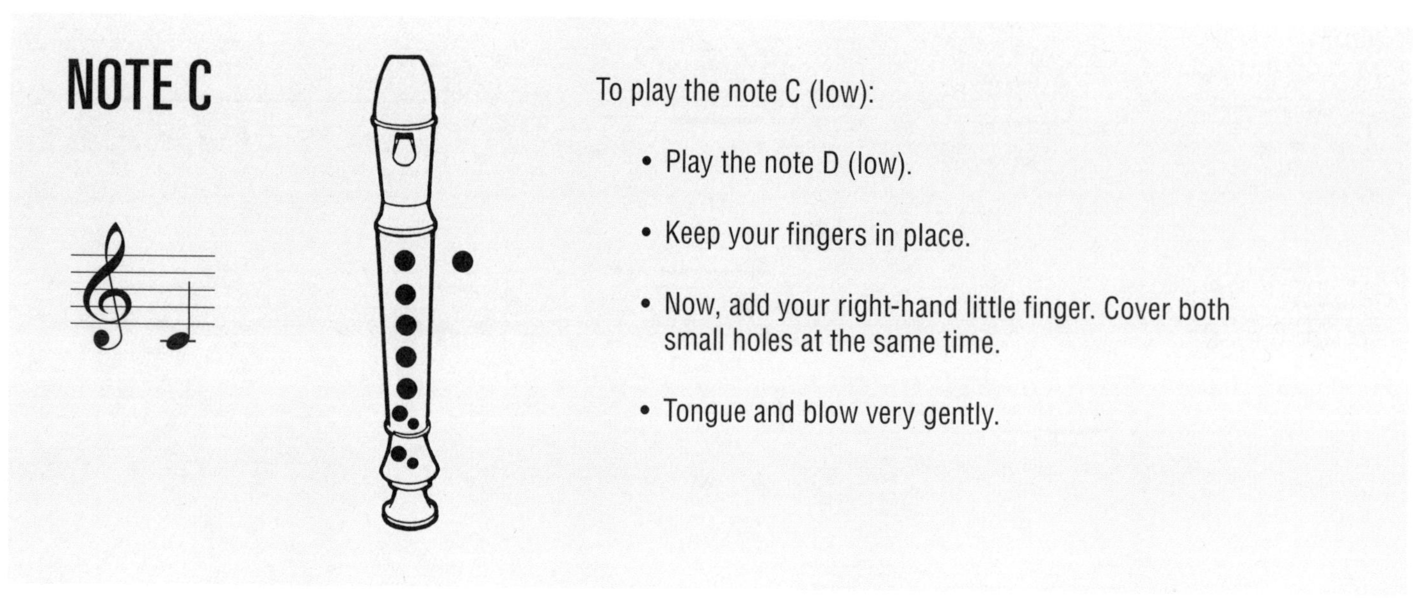

To play the note C (low):

- Play the note D (low).
- Keep your fingers in place.
- Now, add your right-hand little finger. Cover both small holes at the same time.
- Tongue and blow very gently.

ROW, ROW, ROW YOUR BOAT

Just like “Cat in the Plumtree” on page 24, this tune can be played with more than one person. “Player 2” begins when “Player 1” reaches figure 2. Have fun!

WIEGENLIED (LULLABY)

Johannes Brahms

TAKE ME HOME, COUNTRY ROADS

Words and Music by John Denver,
Bill Danoff and Taffy Nivert

OVER TO YOU

- Let's practice your sound. Blow a continuous air stream, as if you are blowing up a balloon.
- You don't need to start and stop your airstream for each note. The tongue will take care of that for you!
- Did you know you can improve the sound of your low notes by blowing "warm" air? Try blowing on your palm as if you were misting up a window. Blowing this way into your recorder will help your low notes to resonate.
- Practice moving between the notes F–low C, to the audio backing track called "Improv on F and C." Choose any rhythmic pattern you like, depending on how confident you are switching between the notes. Perhaps give yourself more time to begin with and then, when you feel more comfortable, increase the frequency of note change. Watch the video to see how you might practice this.
- For more great tips on how to get a lovely sound on your low notes, watch the video lesson dedicated to this technique.

MOON RIVER

Words by Johnny Mercer
Music by Henry Mancini

TRIPLETS

A **triplet** is a group of three notes that should be played in the time of two. Such a grouping is usually indicated by a "3" above or below the beam or notehead. Watch the video lesson to get a practical understanding of how these rhythms work. You can also listen to audio examples of the triplet rhythms below. In example 1, the third beat in each measure contains three eighth notes, rather than two. Together, they equal the length of two standard eighth notes. In the second example, the three triplets take the place of two ordinary quarter notes. Bear in mind that you won't be sounding a note right on beat 4, so it makes more sense to count "three-and-a" right across the two-beat duration of the triplet.

AMAZING GRACE

Words by John Newton
Traditional American Melody

CHARIOTS OF FIRE

from the Feature Film CHARIOTS OF FIRE

By Vangelis

BERGESLUST

Fanny Hensel

FREE TIME

This next piece ("O, Virgo Splendens") does not have bar lines or a time signature. You can play the notes in **free time**, which means away from a strict beat. While you needn't count strictly as you normally would, do use the note values as a guide to how one note relates to another in terms of general length. Try to play each line in one breath, as if chanting a sentence. This is your chance to make the music truly your own, so experiment with different versions and see what you like!

O, VIRGO SPLENDENS

Fourteenth Century Monodic Song

POLKA (PETIT JEAN)

Traditional Dutch Tune

𝄵 CUT TIME

Cut time (also known as "2/2 time" or *alla breve*) is where the half note gets the beat. Here, we count two half-note beats per measure as opposed to four quarter notes. Generally, music in cut time (2/2) is a little quicker than music in 4/4. The time signature for cut time can also written as a "C," bisected with a vertical line. Watch the video for a bit more detail.

HUMORESQUE

Antonín Dvořák

ALLA BREVE

Johann Joachim Quantz

THEME FROM "JURASSIC PARK"

from the Universal Motion Picture JURASSIC PARK

Composed by John Williams

NOTE B♭

To play the note B♭:

- Play the note G.
- Lift up your left middle finger. At the same time, add on your right-hand first finger.
- This is the fingering for the note B♭.
- There is an alternative fingering for this note, which is seen in the upper recorder image and discussed in the video lesson.

♭ THE FLAT SIGN

This is a flat sign. It is a type of accidental. A flat sign lowers the pitch of a note by a half step. If you spot a flat sign before the B note, it means you should play B♭. You can see this in action during "Aura Lee." You might also see the B♭ sign written as a key signature at the very beginning of a piece of music. This means whenever you see a B note in the music, you should play a B♭.

Check out the video lesson on this for greater detail. For a review of all accidentals, watch the video lesson on this topic from page 44.

AURA LEE

Words by W.W. Fosdick
Music by George R. Poulton

Check the key signature. Is this the note B or the note B♭?

DYNAMIC CONTRAST

On sheet music, **dynamic** markings indicate where we should play loudly or softly. When playing the recorder this is achieved by subtly blowing more, or less, air. Watch the video lesson to get a clearer perspective on how to articulate dynamics.

f = **forte** (strong/loud)

p = **piano** (soft/quiet)

It's important to remember that dynamic markings are all relative and not set, predetermined volume levels. "Forte" could be quite different according to certain contexts, such as the performance venue and the style of music being played. Articulating dynamics on the recorder is also not as straightforward as simply blowing a lot more or a lot less into your instrument. Watch the video lesson to pick up a few super tips.

SAILING

Words and Music by Gavin Sutherland

WATER IN THE MOONLIGHT

Thomas Wiggins

CHACONNE

from THE FAIRY QUEEN

Henry Purcell

MODERATE DYNAMICS

Sometimes, music demands a subtlety that goes beyond merely juxtaposing strong and soft playing. Towards this end, "medium" or **mezzo** dynamic markings direct us to play somewhere in between loud and soft.

mf = **mezzo forte** (moderately strong/loud)

mp = **mezzo piano** (moderately soft/quiet)

MY HEART WILL GO ON (LOVE THEME FROM 'TITANIC')

from the Paramount and Twentieth Century Fox Motion Picture TITANIC

Music by James Horner
Lyric by Will Jennings

OVER TO YOU

In this video lesson we only use two notes, F# and B♭. Listen to what I play and then copy me! The "call and response" will help your fingers to get used to these two notes. We'll be playing to a wonderful samba-style track that you can also stream and download for your practice!

COME AGAIN, SWEET LOVE

John Dowland

Flowing

mp

7

mf

13

p

"Come Again, Sweet Love" was written during the period of western European music known as the Renaissance (c.1450–1600). Dynamic markings are not found on printed music from this time; it would have been up to the performer to shape them. The dynamics in your music are just one example of what could be done! Notice in this next piece that each time a section repeats, you need to play it at a different dynamic level. This will add interest to your interpretation.

BRETON DANCE

Traditional Breton Folk Dance

Full of character

f (2° *p*)

5

9

p (2° *f*)

13

GAME OF THRONES

Theme from the HBO Series GAME OF THRONES

THEME FROM TETRIS (KOROBEINIKI)

Russian Folksong

BARBIE GIRL

Words and Music by Claus Norreen, Soren Rasted, Lene Nystrom, Rene Dif, Johnny Pederson and Karsten Delgado

WE ARE THE CHAMPIONS

Words and Music by Freddie Mercury

NOTE E (HIGH)

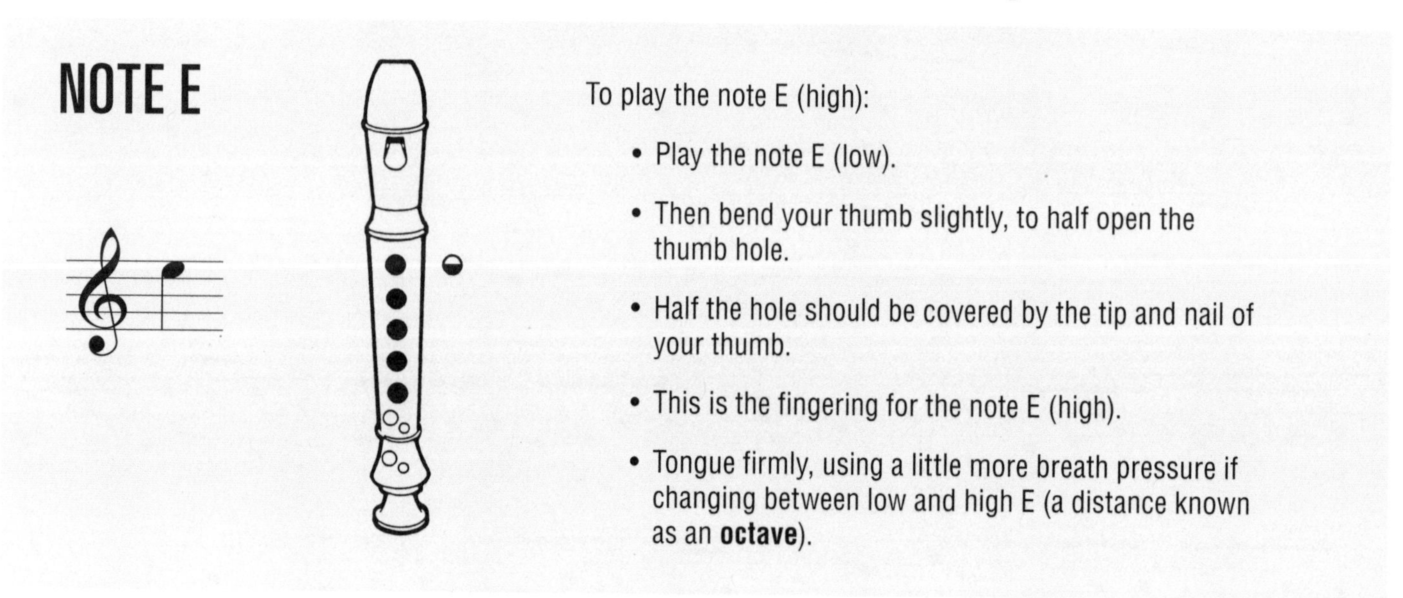

NOTE E

To play the note E (high):

- Play the note E (low).
- Then bend your thumb slightly, to half open the thumb hole.
- Half the hole should be covered by the tip and nail of your thumb.
- This is the fingering for the note E (high).
- Tongue firmly, using a little more breath pressure if changing between low and high E (a distance known as an **octave**).

HALF-HOLING AND NO SQUEAKS!

Sounding the high E note in this way is known as playing a **pinched note**. This can be tricky to get used to but don't worry, watching the video lesson will help your playing to become more reliable.

We've already learned this tune back on page 10. This time, we are incorporating the high E note!

CHEESE AND PICKLE II (DUET)

HELOÍSA

Chiquinha Gonzaga

DO YOU WANT TO BUILD A SNOWMAN?

from FROZEN

Music and Lyrics by Kristen Anderson-Lopez
and Robert Lopez

SUMMERTIME

from PORGY AND BESS®

Music and Lyrics by George Gershwin,
DuBose and Dorothy Heyward and Ira Gershwin

Relaxed and easy

JUPITER

Gustav Holst

Stately

Rubato is derived from an Italian term meaning "to rob!" In music, it refers to the stealing of time by subtly slowing down or speeding up certain passages. Musicians use rubato to add even greater expression to their interpretation. Experiment with this idea while learning the classic Bill Withers song "Ain't No Sunshine." There's no right or wrong; record your various interpretations, listen back, and see what you like best!

AIN'T NO SUNSHINE

Words and Music by Bill Withers

OVER TO YOU

- Choose any piece from pages 8–19.
- Try playing it again but this time half-holing the thumb so it sounds an octave higher.
- Focusing your airstream can help improve your sound. To achieve this, try blowing on your palm in the same way you might blow on hot food to cool it down. This way of blowing "cold" air works well for high notes.

IN DULCI JUBILO

Fourteenth Century German Melody

TRILLS

tr

- A **trill** is a type of **ornament**. Ornaments are used to decorate melodies, making them sound more interesting. In certain classical styles, a trill is often played on the penultimate note of the piece.
- Trills can be played in different ways. We will learn the "Baroque" style, which is commonly encountered in recorder repertoire.
- A trill is played by rapdily moving back and forth between two adjacent notes.
- The trill begins on the beat, not before.
- We start a trill on the note immediately higher than the main notehead above which the trill sign is placed. We then move down to this main note.
- Watch the video to see how to action these lovely ornaments and decorate your melodic lines!

Now that you know how to play trills, you can revisit the following previous pieces and add a trill to the penultimate note!

- "Spring" on page 42
- "Alla Breve" on page 55
- "Come Again, Sweet Love" on page 59

RONDEAU

from THE FAIRY QUEEN

Henry Purcell

SHEEP MAY SAFELY GRAZE

Johann Sebastian Bach

MADRIGAL (DUET)

Mélanie Bonis

Gracefully

MISTER SANDMAN

Lyric and Music by Pat Ballard

ENHARMONIC NOTES

Enharmonic notes sound the same but are written differently on the staff.

B♭ = A♯

Here, we see two different notes but their pitch is exactly the same. Looking at the notes on a piano keyboard makes this clearer.

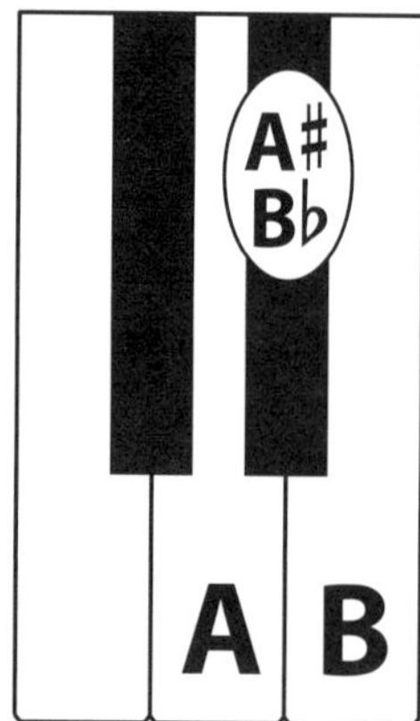

We can see that B♭ and A♯ occupy the same black key on the piano keyboard. They sound at the same pitch. So, when you meet the note A♯ in "In the Hall of the Mountain King," you just play the fingering for a B♭.

GRADUAL DYNAMIC CHANGE

Rather than just suddenly arriving at a dynamic level, it might be more musical to incrementally get louder or softer. On sheet music, **hairpin** dynamic symbols specify the passages of music within which these gradual changes occur.

Think of hairpin symbols as representing the shape of your mouth.

Imagine saying the words "I am getting louder!" Begin with a whisper and gradually get louder until you are shouting. As you get louder, your mouth gets wider, just like the **crescendo** hairpin.

I am getting louder!

Now, imagine saying the words "I am getting softer." Begin by shouting and gradually get quieter until you end the sentence in a whisper. As you get softer, your mouth gets narrower, just like the **decrescendo** hairpin.

I am getting softer.

IN THE HALL OF THE MOUNTAIN KING

from PEER GYNT

NOTE C♯ (HIGH)

To play the note C♯ (high):

- Play the note D (high).
- Keep your fingers in place.
- Then, add the first left-hand finger.
- This is the fingering for the note C♯ (high).

We've played this epic rock song before using different notes! Now, try it using your new note C♯ (high).

SEPTEMBER

Words and Music by Maurice White,
Al McKay and Allee Willis

You might see the C-sharp sign represented within a key signature. In this case, whenever you come across the notes F or C in the music, play the notes F♯ and C♯.

PHRASE MARKS

A **phrase** is like a musical sentence. Every melodic phrase has a natural beginning, middle, and end, just like a good written sentence. Phrases are often indicated on sheet music by **phrase marks**, which are curved lines above or below groups of notes. In "Arabesque," the phrase marks indicate that you should tongue the notes smoothly, imagining a clear beginning and end to each phrase.

ARABESQUE

Josephine Lang

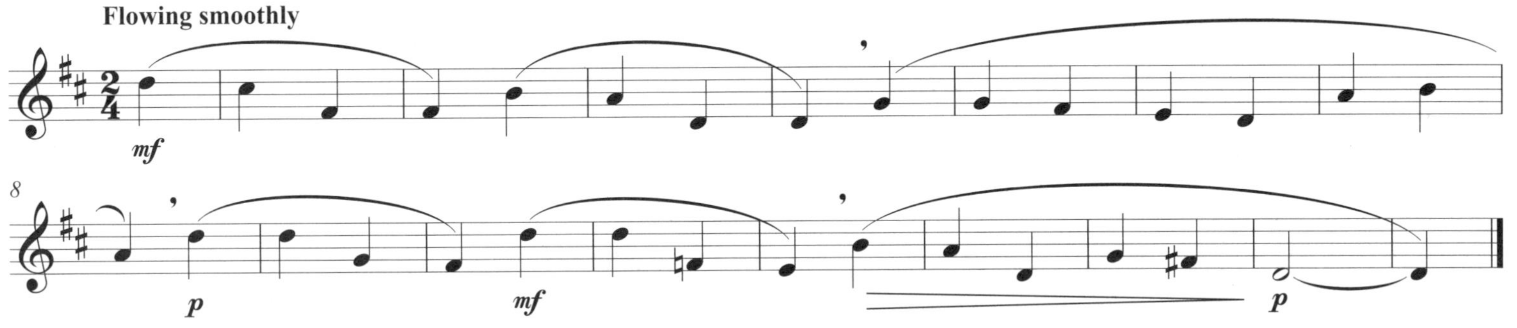

BALI HA'I
from SOUTH PACIFIC

Lyrics by Oscar Hammerstein II
Music by Richard Rodgers

RECORDER PROBLEMS 101

Learning the recorder is incredibly fun and rewarding. But it can be frustrating when you hit a problem that's tricky to solve. In this video we'll troubleshoot the most common recorder problems and how to fix them, including:

- "The notes are squeaking."
- "I can't reach the holes."
- "I'm running out of air."
- "My playing sounds clunky."
- "My recorder is clogged up."

The composer Einaudi says this piece should be played *Andante con moto*. This basically means at a moderately slow speed but with movement. In other words, reflective but not too slow!

LE ONDE

Ludovico Einaudi

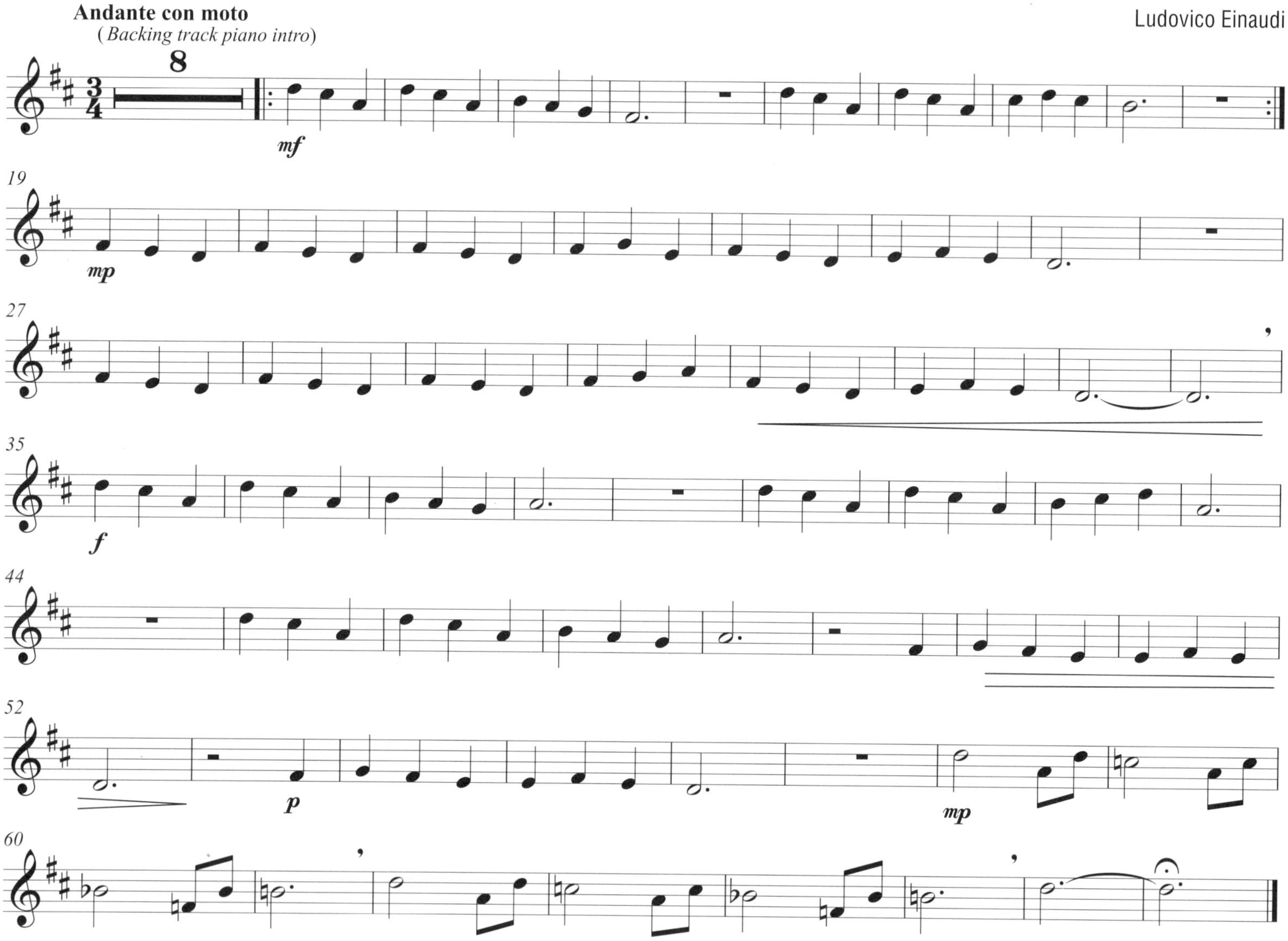
Andante con moto
(Backing track piano intro)
8
mf
19
mp
27
35
f
44
52
p
mp
60

CAN-CAN

from ORPHEUS IN THE UNDERWORLD

Jacques Offenbach

Brilliantly, with fun
f
5

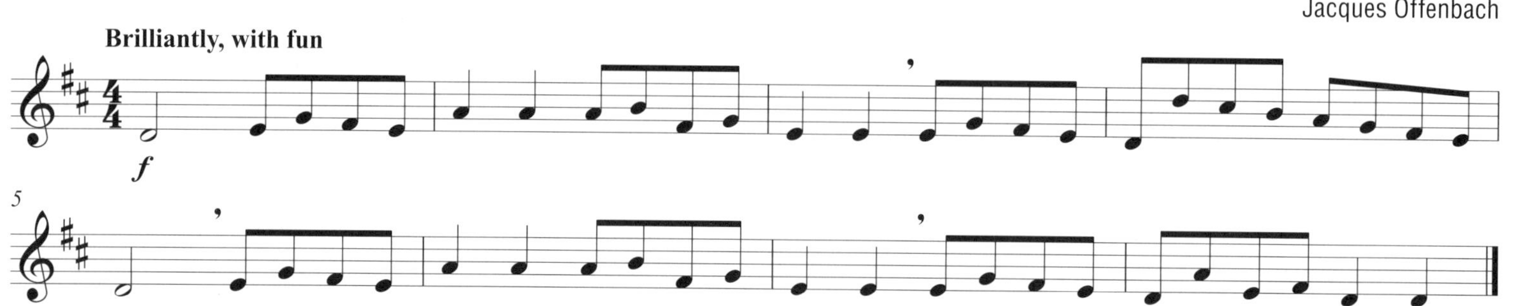

OVER TO YOU

Inventing (or **composing**) your own music can be simple if you know where to start and a great way of developing your playing, too! Watch the video for guidance with:

- Getting started.
- Devising your own musical material.
- Creating a structure for your music.

In 9/8 time, there are nine eighth notes per measure. We count them in groups of three like this: "one-and-ah, two-and-ah, three-and-ah."

FOXHUNTER'S JIG

Traditional Folk Tune

Dynamic markings have been deliberately omitted from this piece. Try creating some of your own, following the line of the music to see what fits. There's no right or wrong; you should just experiment and find your favorite interpretation. What impact do your dynamic changes have on the music?

LORD WILLOUGHBY'S WELCOME HOME

MINUET

ACCENTS

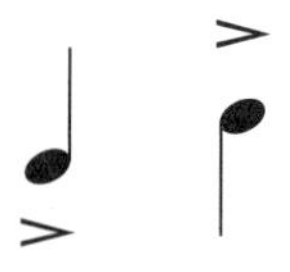

An **accent** is another type of articulation. Accents are indicated by a > sign above or below a notehead. It means to play the note with extra force. On the recorder, we do this with a sharp tongue stroke. You can have a go at this in the next group of pieces, starting with "We Don't Talk About Bruno" from Disney's *Encanto*. But before you begin this, review all your articulation types side-by-side in the video lesson entitled "Articulation."

WE DON'T TALK ABOUT BRUNO

from ENCANTO

Music and Lyrics by Lin-Manuel Miranda

SINFONIA II

Leonora Duarte

TOAD IN A MOLE HOLE (IN D)

OVER TO YOU

On page 47, we experimented with recording our playing and using that to inform our practice. Have a listen back to this recording. Pick out some areas of your playing that you can hear have improved. Well done, that's progress! Now, choose one thing you'd like to work on further. Don't try to fix too much at once and enjoy the process of developing your recorder playing.

CONCERT PROGRAM

The next five pieces comprise a spread of folk music, classical favorites, jazz, and popular song. What better way to celebrate your journey on the recorder than to perform these together as a mini concert with backing audio, in front of friends and family!

MORRISON'S JIG

Traditional

This arrangement is from a song first published in 1602, retelling the Greek myth of Amaryllis. There are no dynamic markings. Follow the melodic line, listen to the backing audio, and decide where the music should build up and ebb away. Perhaps be inspired by the original story, which tells us how the infatuated maiden Amaryllis would pierce her heart with a golden arrow each day and wander to the cottage of her love Alteo, shedding drops of blood that eventually formed into the eponymous scarlet flower.

AMARILLI MIA BELLA

Jacob van Eyck

Tenderly, with movement

IT COULD HAPPEN TO YOU

from the Paramount Picture AND THE ANGELS SING

Words by Johnny Burke
Music by James Van Heusen

O, FRONDE CARE

Rosa Giacinta Badalla

I KNEW YOU WERE TROUBLE

Words and Music by Taylor Swift,
Shellback and Max Martin

NEXT STEPS

THE RECORDER FAMILY

Did you know that the recorder is not just one instrument but a whole family of different sizes and models?

The recorder has been around for centuries and it has changed a great deal over time. From the shape of the inner bore to the addition of keys, all of these variables can serve to alter the sound. The recorder exists in a wide range of sizes, from the tiny "garklein," to a giant "sub-bass." And larger recorders are still being developed! Historical recorders can be built in a range of keys, pitches, and tuning systems to more authentically perform music from the past. You can even 3D-print recorders to precisely match historic designs. The possibilities are endless!

Watch this video to see and hear some of the members of this special family, and to find out what you could use each instrument for.

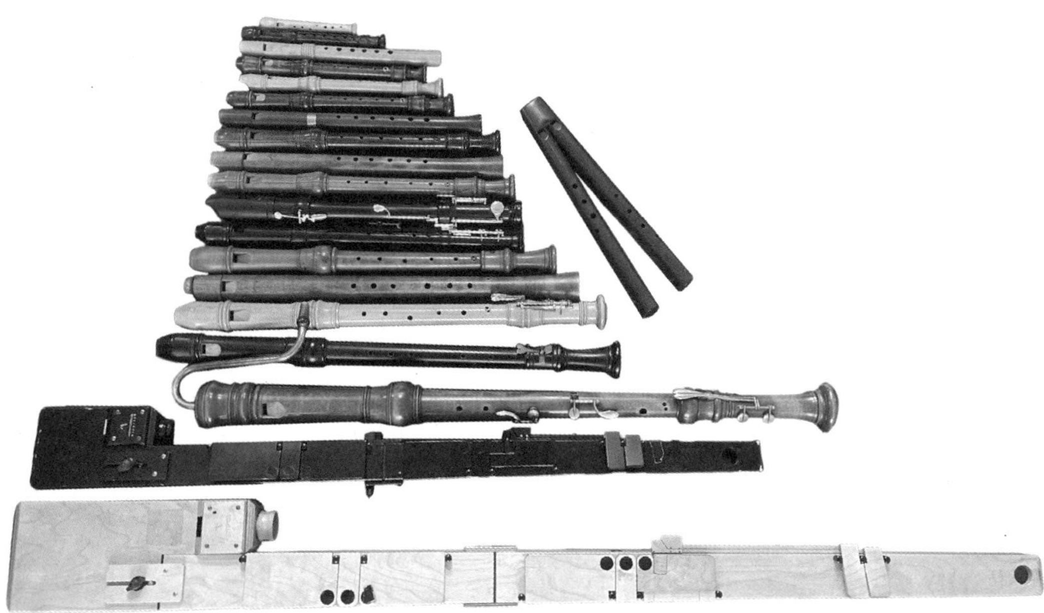

(From top to bottom): Garklein in C; Sopranino in F; Ganassi Soprano in C; Soprano in C at 442Hz; Soprano in C at 415Hz; "Fourth flute" soprano in B♭; Transitional G alto; F alto at 442Hz; Consort F alto at 466Hz; F alto at 415Hz; "Eagle" modern F alto; "Modern" F alto with E foot; "Voice flute" in D; Consort C tenor at 466Hz; Tenor in C; "Fourth flute" tenor in B♭; Basset recorder in F; Great bass in C; (right) Medieval double flute.

BEYOND THIS BOOK

You now have a good range of notes at your fingertips and the knowledge you need to get started on your favorite music. But what else is out there? Watch my goodbye video and get some ideas to keep your inspiration flowing.